MAPS & GLOBES

MAPS & GLOBES

BY
JACK KNOWLTON

PICTURES BY
HARRIETT BARTON

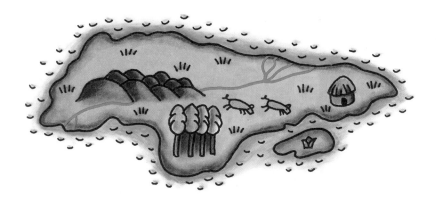

Thomas Y. Crowell   New York

Library of Congress Cataloging in Publication Data
Knowlton, Jack.
    Maps and globes.

    Summary: A brief history of mapmaking, a simple
explanation of how to read maps and globes, and an
introduction to the many different kinds of maps there
are.
    1. Maps—Juvenile literature.   2. Globes—Juvenile
literature. [1. Maps. 2. Globes] I. Barton, Harriett,
ill.   II. Title.
GA105.6.K58 1985   912   85-47537
ISBN 0-690-04457-7
ISBN 0-690-04459-3 (lib. bdg.)

For our mothers

Harriett Botts Wyatt
and
Josephine O'Gorman Knowlton

The very first maps were just scratches in dirt or sand.

Thousands of years ago, our ancestors invented the map.

Ancient maps were crude but very useful tools.
They helped people find food, clean water,
and the way back home—even when
home was a deep, dark cave.

Babylonian clay tablet

Chinese silk map

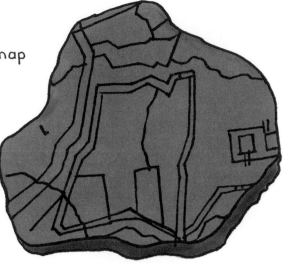
Ancient city map
drawn in clay

As civilizations grew, better maps were needed.

The oldest existing maps are from the ancient desert kingdom of Babylonia. These maps were etched on tablets of damp clay that soon baked rock hard in the midday sun.

Early Chinese mapmakers painted beautiful maps of their empire on pure silk cloth. People in every part of the world cleverly used local materials to make the maps they wanted and needed.

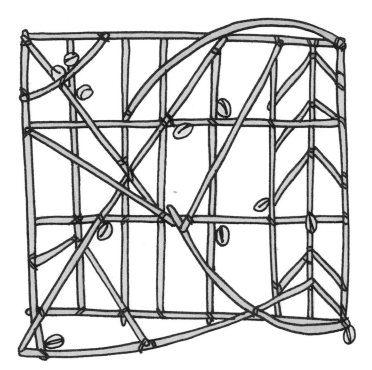

Charts are maps used to sail the wide oceans.

The Polynesian Islanders sailed the vast Pacific Ocean using *stick chart* maps. These charts were woven with reeds and palm leaves that showed the ocean's currents and wave directions. Seashells were attached to each chart to indicate the larger islands.

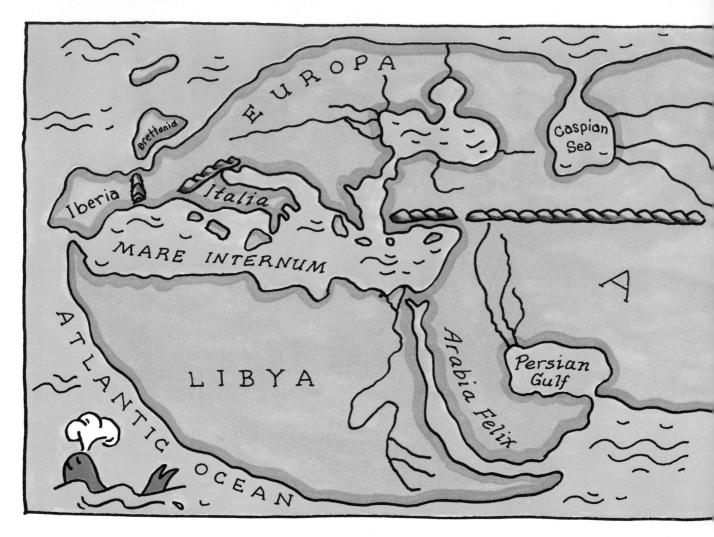

But ancient *world maps* were incredibly incomplete.

Until a few centuries ago, the earth was neither fully explored nor accurately mapped. As a result, these maps presented a world that looked like this...an incomplete and very incorrect world!

At this time, most people still believed that the earth was as flat as a pancake. If it really was flat, then ships and sailors might tumble over the edge if they sailed too far from dry land!

The Age of Exploration begins... Columbus sails.

About 500 years ago, some big changes were in the wind. Brave sailors and mapmakers were beginning to sail farther and farther from the safe shores of Europe. The true shape, the true look of the earth was about to be discovered. Realistic, dependable maps would soon follow.

When Christopher Columbus sailed west in 1492,
he was actually looking for the Spice Islands of India.
He wanted to discover a safe, short ocean route from
Spain to India and back again. What he really found
proved to be two unmapped continents—North
and South America.

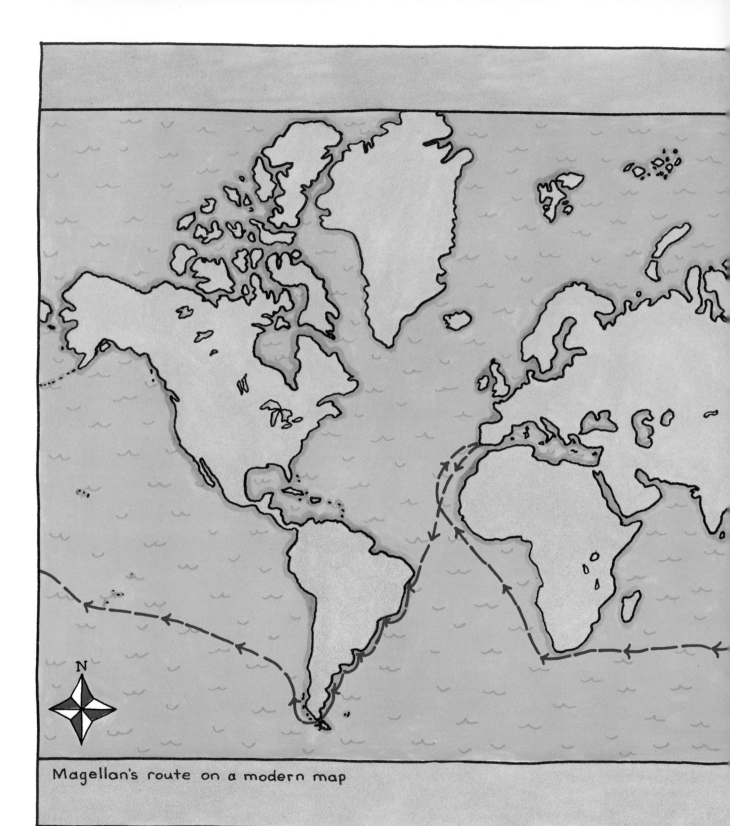

Magellan's route on a modern map

Magellan sails...and *proves* that the earth is round.

In 1519, Ferdinand Magellan sailed from Spain with a fleet of five ships. Magellan wanted to be the first explorer to sail all the way around the world. If the voyage was successful, it would prove to one and all that the earth was round. The fleet sailed down through the icy waters at the tip of South America, across the Pacific and Indian Oceans, around Africa's Cape of Good Hope, and back to Spain.

After three long years at sea, one battered surviving ship had completely encircled the earth. An explosion of discovery and exploration was soon underway now that all were convinced that the earth was round. Like an orange. Like a cannonball. Like a globe.

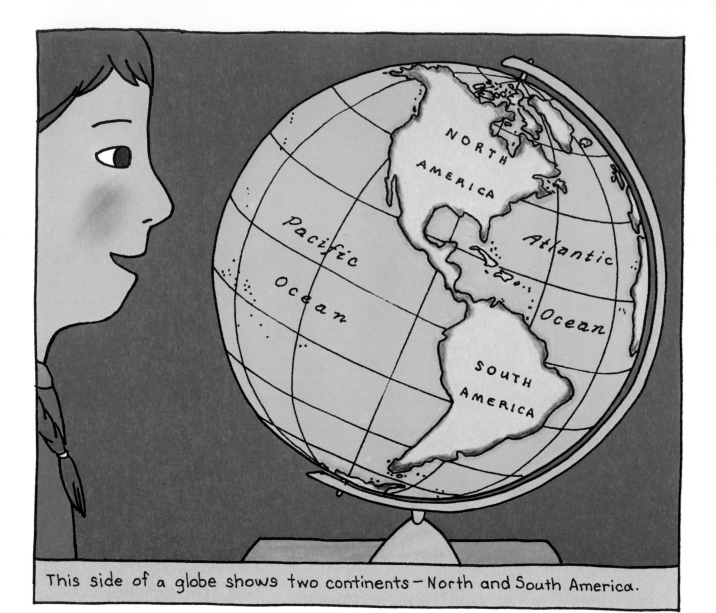

This side of a globe shows two continents—North and South America.

Globes are tiny models of our earth.

Globes (unlike flat maps) are shaped exactly like the earth—like a ball or *sphere.* They are very tiny models—the earth is really 30 to 40 million times

Rotate a globe and find the widest splash of blue — that's the Pacific Ocean. The Pacific is the biggest place on earth by far.

bigger than the globe in your classroom.

Globes, because they are round, put all the world's geography in its proper place; they give the truest possible view of the whole earth.

Maps put our round earth on flat paper.

Maps are precisely drawn pictures of the earth—pictures of the *entire* earth or *any part* of it. There are maps of the world, maps of the country where you live, and maps of your hometown. Maps put all the wet oceans and all the lumpy, bumpy land on sheets of nice, flat, dry paper.

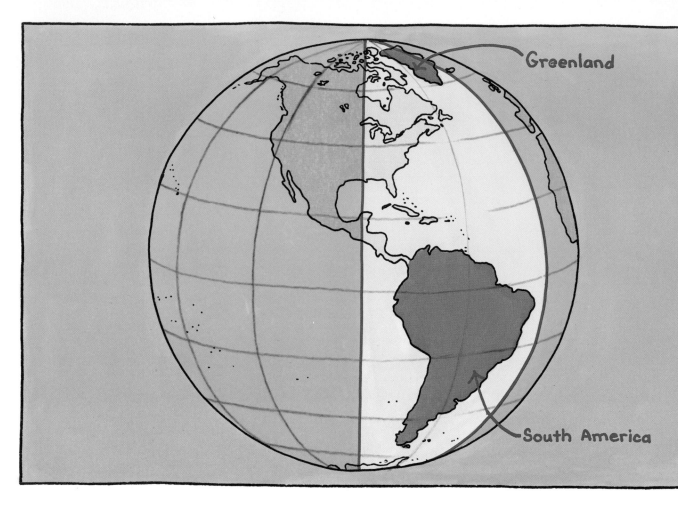

Globes are the most realistic world maps.

Since globes duplicate the true round shape of the earth, all distances, directions, sizes, and shapes are *true-to-scale* on globes.

But maps must artificially flatten the real round world, so mapmakers cut, stretch, and distort some parts of the earth to get it all flat on paper.

16

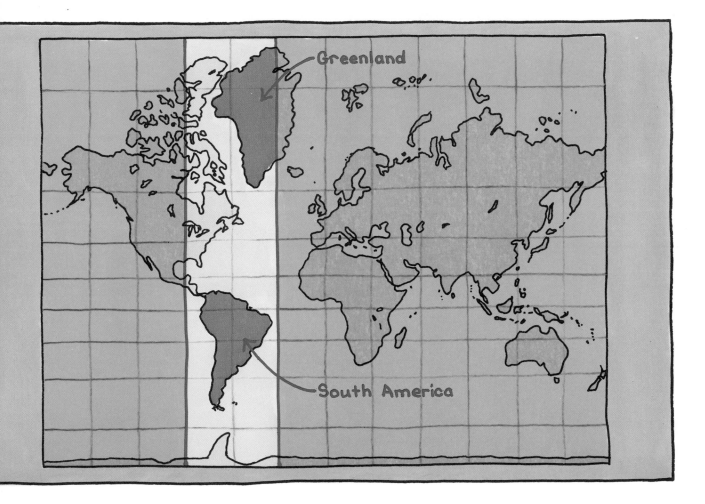

The worst map distortion is at the top and bottom of the world—in the Arctic and Antarctic. Greenland, for instance, looks bigger than all of South America on a flat map. But it isn't. A globe instantly shows that South America is really much bigger. In fact, it's eight times bigger!

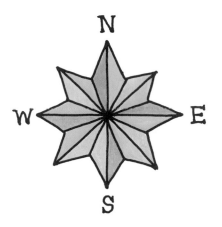

Maps have a language you can learn.

Maps and globes can take you places and show you things when you know how to read them! *Map language* is partly names and numbers. It's also bright colors, great circles, imaginary lines, and tiny symbolic cartoons. Map language begins with the four basic directions. *Direction* means which way.

North is the direction toward the North Pole from any other place on earth. *South* is just the opposite—it's always toward the South Pole. *East* is the direction where the sun appears every morning, and *West* is toward the sunset.

The Equator divides the earth in half.

The *Equator* is a great imaginary line around the middle of the earth. It divides the earth into two equal parts—the *Northern* and the *Southern Hemispheres.*

A *hemisphere* is exactly one half of a sphere.

The Northern Hemisphere is the half that's north of (or above) the Equator. Most of the world's dry land and most of its people are within this area.

The Southern Hemisphere is everywhere south of (or below) the Equator. Of the seven continents on earth, only two, Australia and Antarctica, are completely within the Southern Hemisphere.

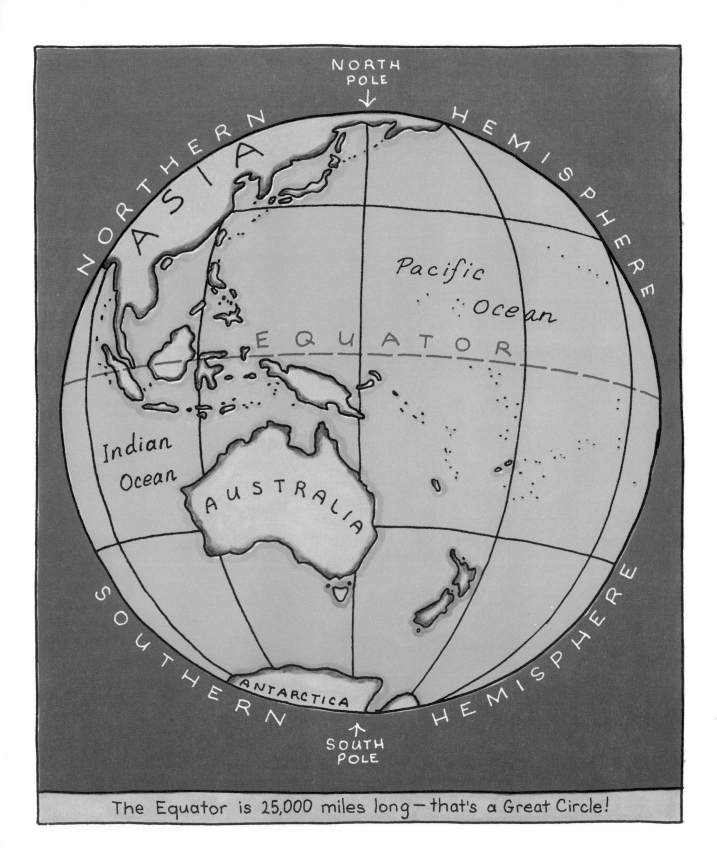

The Equator is 25,000 miles long—that's a Great Circle!

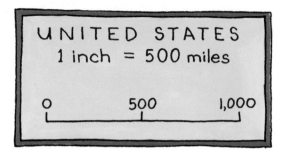

How to put big countries on small pieces of paper.

Distance is how far apart places are. Maps and globes miniaturize the actual distances—they are *drawn to scale.*

Scale is the system that reduces the real land, the real oceans to sizes that fit on paper. Scale lets you hold millions of square miles in your own two hands.

To find distances on this map: (1) measure the inches with a ruler, and (2) multiply by 500. The map distance between San Diego and Boston is about 5 inches, so the real distance is about 2,500 miles.

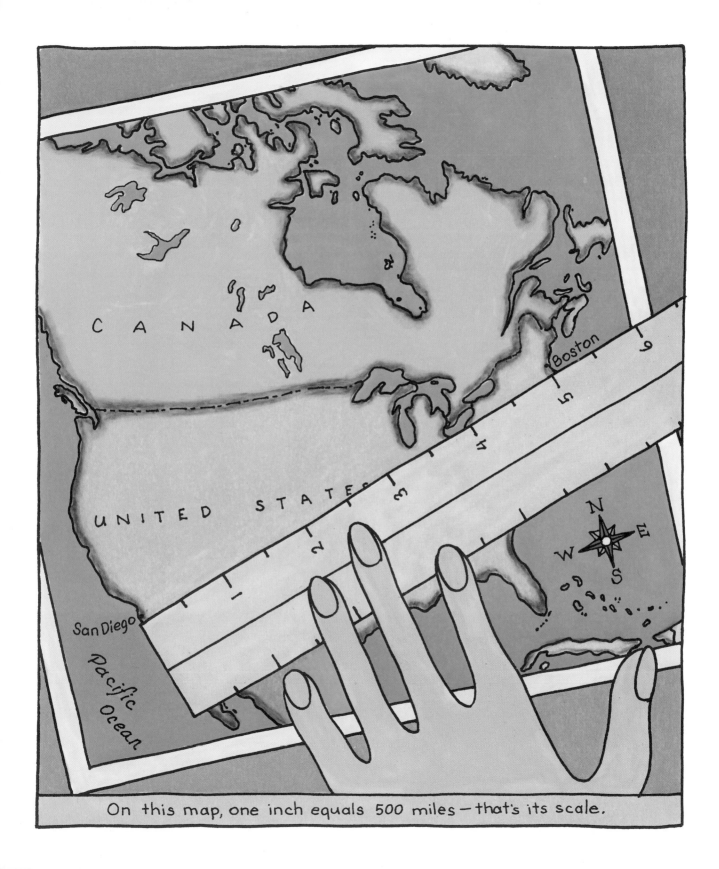

On this map, one inch equals 500 miles—that's its scale.

You can measure the earth with a piece of string.

Globes differ in size, so they differ in scale. The exact scale of any globe is shown in its *key* or *legend.* To find mileage on a globe: (1) measure the inches with a string, then (2) multiply by the scale.

For instance, the shortest jet route from Chicago to Calcutta, India, would be due north over the North Pole. This 'Great Circle Route' is a long, curving distance of about 8,000 miles.

The scale on a twelve-inch globe is about one inch to 675 miles.

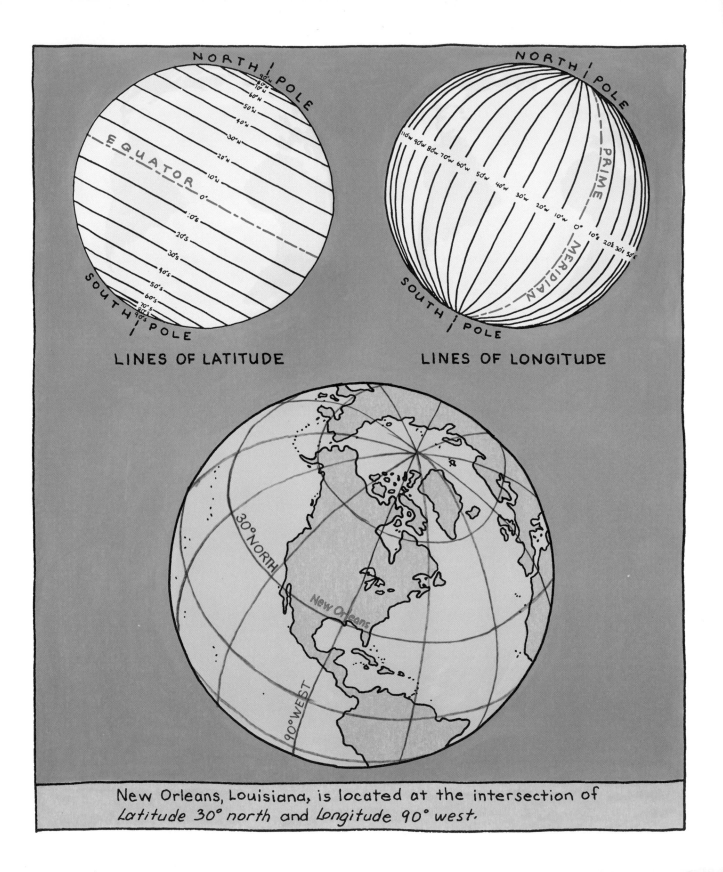

LINES OF LATITUDE

LINES OF LONGITUDE

New Orleans, Louisiana, is located at the intersection of *Latitude 30° north* and *Longitude 90° west.*

Where on earth am I....exactly?

Maps use a network of intersecting imaginary lines to identify the exact location of every place on earth. This network builds from three locations that we already know—the North Pole, the South Pole, and the Equator.

Latitudes (or *Parallels*) tell how far north or south. Lines of latitude are drawn parallel to the Equator. They measure the *degrees* (°) north or south of it. The Equator itself is zero latitude—it's exactly in the middle.

Longitudes (or *Meridians*) tell how far east or west. Meridians are imaginary lines running vertically from the North Pole to the South Pole. East and west are measured in degrees from the Greenwich or Prime Meridian.

How high are the mountains?

Elevation means how high. Elevation tells you the *altitude* of any place on land—mountains, valleys, deserts, and glaciers. Elevation is measured from *sea level*. Sea level is considered zero elevation.

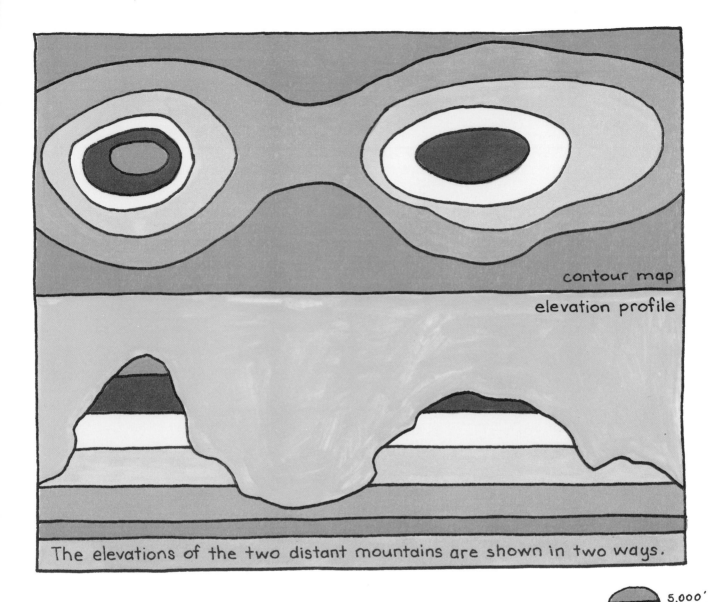

contour map

elevation profile

The elevations of the two distant mountains are shown in two ways.

5,000'
4,000'
3,000'
2,000'
1,000'
SEA LEVEL

Mapmakers combine colors and contour lines to highlight the location, shape, and elevation of especially high places. The highest place on earth is Mount Everest in the Himalayas. Its peak is 29,028 feet above sea level.

How deep are the oceans?

Depth means how deep or how far it is to the bottom. Depths are measured from sea level (zero depth) straight down to the bottom of the ocean, the sea, the lake. Mapmakers use contour lines and several shades of blue to show the depths and features on an ocean floor.

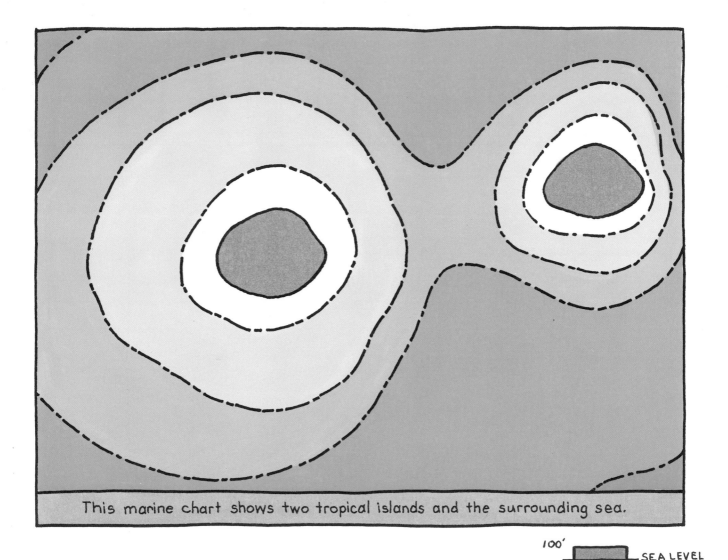

This marine chart shows two tropical islands and the surrounding sea.

100'

SEA LEVEL
100'
200'
300'
400'
500'

There are more mountains and volcanoes
under the oceans than on dry land! Deep canyons
split the ocean floors. The deepest—the Mariana
Trench—is 36,198 feet below sea level. That's about 7
times deeper than the Grand Canyon in Arizona!

Physical maps— the nature of places.

There are many kinds of maps. Each provides a different type of information.

Physical maps present the works of nature. They show the vegetation, terrain, and other natural features of such places as jungles, deserts, and open grasslands.

Physical maps show the elevation of the terrain; they also note the *depressions,* which are areas of land that lie below sea level.

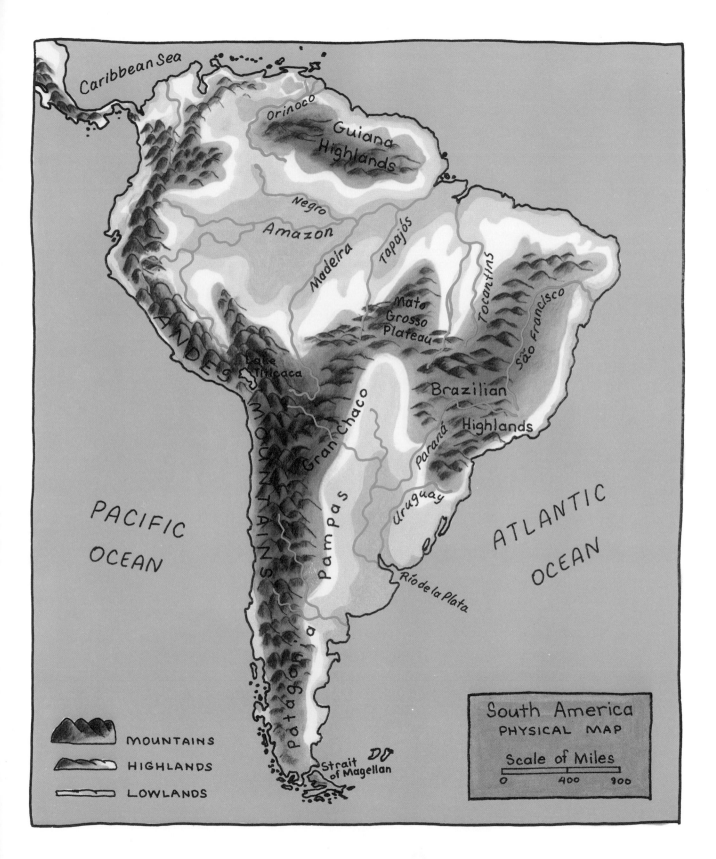

Political maps—people and countries.

There are over 150 independent countries or nations on earth. *Political maps* show the capital cities and the boundaries between countries.

Boundaries or *international borders* reflect the political divisions that people have agreed to.

Some borders are straight lines plotted by surveyors. Other borders follow natural features—some run along the highest peaks in a mountain range.

Still others are plotted precisely down the middle of large rivers, so that each country gets one riverbank and precisely one half of the river!

Caribbean Sea

VENEZUELA
⊛ Caracas

GUYANA
⊛ Georgetown
SURINAME
⊛ Paramaribo
FRENCH GUIANA
⊛ Cayenne

⊛ Bogatá
COLUMBIA

Quito ⊛
EQUADOR

PERU

B R A Z I L

Lima ⊛

La Paz
⊛
BOLIVIA
⊛ Sucre

⊛ Brasília

PACIFIC

OCEAN

PARAGUAY

Asuncíon ⊛

ATLANTIC

OCEAN

A R G E N T I N A

Santiago ⊛

URUGUAY
⊛ Montevideo

Buenos Aires

South America
POLITICAL MAP
Capital Cities ⊛

Scale of Miles

0   400   800

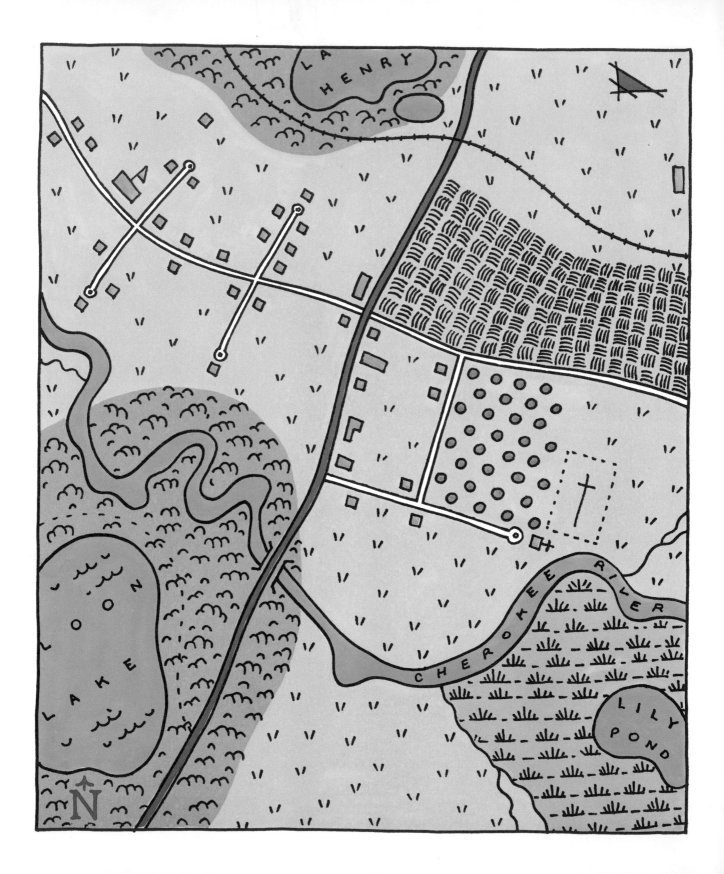

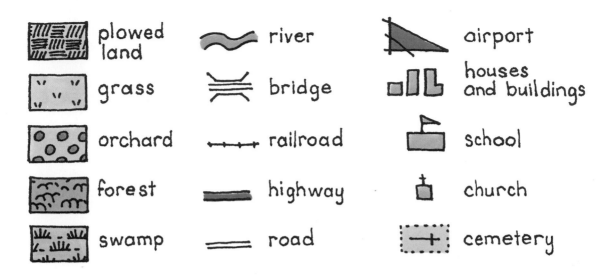

Local maps—getting closer to home.

Local maps show you smaller areas. Each gives a detailed, close-up look at a community and its environment. Local maps show the familiar, natural *features*—the forests, the rivers, the sandy beaches. They also show the *landmarks*, the special features that are big, easy-to-see, and easy-to-remember.

Local maps also show the *cultural* or *man-made* features in the community. Cultural features are the visible evidence of human work and activity upon the earth. They include highways, school buildings, wheat fields, and airports.

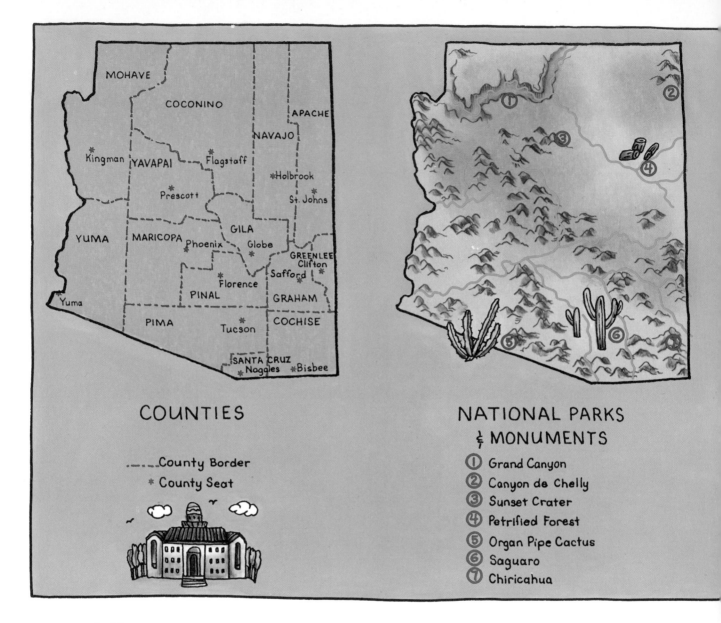

COUNTIES

------ County Border
* County Seat

NATIONAL PARKS
& MONUMENTS
① Grand Canyon
② Canyon de Chelly
③ Sunset Crater
④ Petrified Forest
⑤ Organ Pipe Cactus
⑥ Saguaro
⑦ Chiricahua

There are many ways to see Arizona.

Many maps provide general information about an area's geography—they give an overview of its landscape, landmarks, and features.

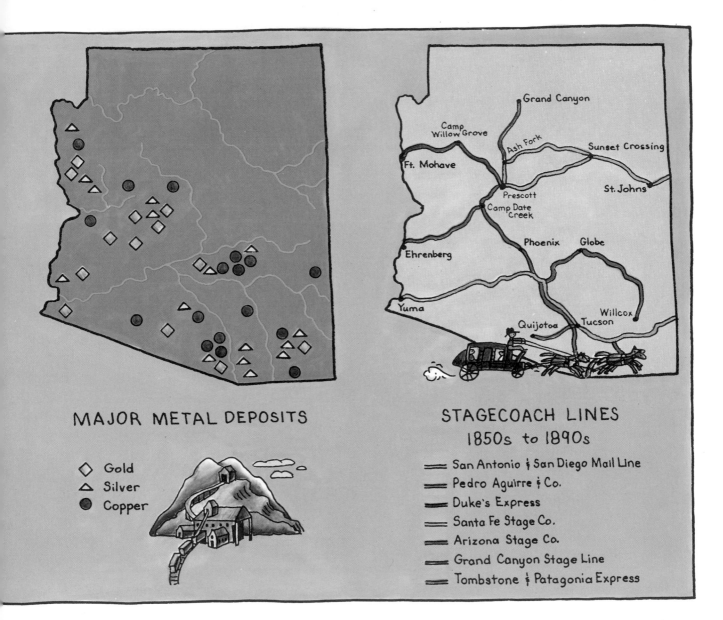

MAJOR METAL DEPOSITS

◇ Gold
△ Silver
● Copper

STAGECOACH LINES
1850s to 1890s

══ San Antonio & San Diego Mail Line
══ Pedro Aguirre & Co.
══ Duke's Express
══ Santa Fe Stage Co.
══ Arizona Stage Co.
══ Grand Canyon Stage Line
══ Tombstone & Patagonia Express

Other maps present specialized information about a place. They focus on a single topic at a time. A few of these topics are population, climate, history, and wildlife.

The world is waiting for you.

If you take a fancy to any place on earth, you can
go there today and still be home in time for dinner!
Just walk into a library, open up an *atlas*, and fly there
in your imagination.

An *atlas* is a book full of maps—it's your personal passport to our wide world. There's a collection of atlases in every library in the land. Their Dewey Decimal Number is 912.

So open a map or spin a globe—
the wide world awaits you.